STEAM MEMORIES: 1950's – 1960's

No. 101: NORTHUMBERLAND BRANCH LINES 3

DAVID DUNN

Copyright Book Law Publications 2018
ISBN 978-1-909625-87-7

INTRODUCTION

This third volume covering the branch lines of Northumberland features two rather long branches out in the countryside, and two shorter branches which were connected to the maritime activities served by the North Eastern Railway and its successors - but not in that order. In *Northumberland Branch Lines 2* we travelled along the line from Alnwick to Alnmouth and now we briefly return to Alnwick in order to traverse the branch to Coldstream; known as the Alnwick & Cornhill Railway but also as the Alnwick & Coldstream. In order to tidy-up the routes around Blyth and bring in the commuter services to and from Newcastle, we travel to Blyth from Manors albeit missing out ground already covered. The virtually unique and somewhat quirky one-mile branch from Trafalgar yard near Manors to the river known as the Quayside branch is presented in its entirety but missing out those sections languishing in perpetual darkness. Finally, the Wansbeck line from Morpeth to Rothbury (the Wannie) will take us back into the country and the quiet open spaces to be found in the 1950s, and even today, on a good day.

It's an eclectic mix but nevertheless interesting; each journey will be explained in captions that will hopefully inform and perhaps entertain.

David Dunn, Cramlington, 2018

Cover J21 No.65033 tops the eight-hundred-odd foot Summit Cottages location on 'the Wannie' whilst working a Morpeth-Woodburn pick-up goods, circa 1952. The 0-6-0 had been climbing continuously since Morpeth but the last four miles or so since Knowesgate had been the stiffest test; it would be time to shut-off soon and then sit back for the descent to Woodburn. *S.C.Crook (ARPT)*.

Previous page Back in Alnwick but this time we'll be taking the route to Coldstream. This undated image shows two prospective spotters' looking at the cameraman in between watching the proceedings of an unidentified Peppercorn K1 (probably No.62006) moving up to its next duty, an Alnmouth departure. The Coldstream trains, before their demise, worked into and out of this particular platform – No.1 – but our mid-60s' photograph reveals that Alnmouth trains now used both platform faces. *Malcolm Dunnett (ARPT)*.

Printed and bound by The Amadeus Press, Cleckheaton, West Yorkshire
First published in the United Kingdom by Book Law Publications, 382 Carlton Hill, Nottingham, NG4 1JA

ALNWICK – COLDSTREAM

This atmospheric image dates from 19th March 1966 and shows Peppercorn K1 No.62011 in the throat of Alnwick station; the view leads us towards the bridge beneath which the line to Coldstream once ran to the right of the lines to Alnmouth. The tall signal box stands like a monument to Victorian enterprise whereby anything, it seems, was possible. *I.S.Carr (ARPT)*.

Alnwick station as seen from beneath the road bridge mentioned in the previous caption. The extensive – and some might say indulgent - facilities at this terminus were quite apparent but were provided just in case a certain family might pop in; sometimes they did! Besides the three-bay train shed over the island platform, an extensive goods yard contained all the necessary facilities, and more, required at a country branch terminus. The terminus was illustrated more fully in *Northumberland Branch Lines:2* so now we'll take our leave and proceed initially in a south-westerly direction over some interesting and dramatic countryside towards the northern border of the county. *J. Mallon (NERA)*.

Now the height of the signal box can be appreciated as it pokes above the road bridge which carried a minor road off the original alignment of the A1 trunk road. At this point the two rail routes leaving Alnwick split with the line to Alnmouth heading south-east on the right whilst our interest lies in the track work immediately to the right of the photographer which would loop around a 360 degrees change-of-direction in the next couple of miles to head north-west briefly before following the contours of the land whilst climbing an arduous 1 in 50 for four miles to Summit. From the location here, which was some 223 feet above sea level, the route climbed 432 feet to the highest point on the line. Our destination, Coldstream – the station serving Cornhill-on-Tweed – was thirty-five miles and forty chains distant or twenty-six as the crow flies! If the weather keeps up it should be plain-sailing all the way. *J. Mallon (NERA).*

This is Summit cutting in 1953. We are looking in the Up direction toward Alnwick; on the left are the remaining stones of the signal box base. Originally a loop – with a capacity to hold a tender engine and ten goods vehicles – was installed here on the opposite side of the line to the box. Closed in 1911, the 14-lever box dated from the opening of the line in 1887 but was abolished when the loop was taken out. It is reported that the weight of the sandstone rock excavated and removed from these cuttings during construction of the line amounted to more than half-a-million tons! Hopefully it found some use elsewhere. *J.W.Armstrong (ARPT).*

(*opposite, top*) Heading in the Up direction, an unidentified D20 and its diminutive load run along the embankment to the west of Edlingham station on a date unrecorded but probably in BR times. The adverse gradient facing the Alnwick bound trains was just the same as those in the Down direction – 1 in 50 – but this 4-4-0 shouldn't have any trouble breasting the summit. The Station Master's house can be seen right of centre. *M.Halbert collection.* (*opposite, bottom*) Looking south-east on a glorious – weather-wise – 27th February 1953 towards Edlingham bridge and along the substantial embankment where the station is tucked away behind the few trees on the hillside. The viaduct consisted of five 40ft. arches with a maximum height of 60ft over the River Aln. It can be discerned in this image that the pier between the second and third arches is much more substantial than the other piers and was constructed such to alleviate foundation problems during building. Although passenger services ceased at the station in 1930, goods and parcels services remained until September 1948 when they too were withdrawn, the first on the line. *J.W.Armstrong (ARPT).*

The view of Hillhead tunnel from the cab of D20 No.62371, 27th February 1953; located just north of milepost 8, the bore was 351 yards long and was the only tunnel on the route. This is the northern end of the bore with the 4-4-0 climbing a 1 in 66 gradient. *J.W.Armstrong (ARPT).*

Ten miles done and the weather is holding. This is Whittingham station at 1215hrs on Friday 27th February 1953 looking north. Located some one and a half miles east from the village it was named after (pop. 437 in 1937), the station was built next to the A697 road to which the railway would run alongside for the next fourteen miles. Like all the stations on the line, Whittingham was substantially built but it was also equipped with all the necessary facilities including goods shed, sidings, and at opening it served a brick works which stood behind the signal box. The island platform enabled trains to pass each other without the need to use passing loops. *J.W.Armstrong (ARPT).*

A view after the cessation of operations on the line in 1953! The deserted signal box (nineteen levers, three spare) was decommissioned shortly after the last trains ran at this end of the route; note the name board still in situ. The station had been closed from 22nd September 1930 but remained very much intact and the clock was still wound! Now it appears that wagons have been placed along the line to carry away equipment and assets for further use or salvage. The tree gives us a clue as to which way the prevailing wind travels! *J.W.Armstrong (ARPT)*.

(*right*) With its mixed train, D20 No.62371 takes water at Whittingham on 27th February 1953. *J.W.Armstrong (ARPT)*.

(*left*) Another view of the D20 with the crew preparing for departure, back to Alnwick. *J.W.Armstrong (ARPT)*.

Just over a mile later we come across the next station along which is Glanton. Again the village after which it was named is some distance away to the west although at three-quarters of a mile it's nearer than the last. Note the original signal box boarded-up; it was replaced in 1901 by a dwarf frame located in the wooden building on the platform to the left. We are looking north in the Down direction on the main line whilst the station platform is served by the loop. Closure of Glanton station took place 22nd September 1930. *J. Mallon (NERA).*

(*opposite*) Whilst working what became the penultimate parcels train over the southern end of the line, No.62371 runs round its stock after a bit of shunting at Hedgeley on 27th February 1953; the signalman can be seen handing over the staff to the crew. The 4-4-0 had worked from Alnwick tender first and will continue as such to Ilderton where for the return journey it would tun smokebox first for a bit more comfort on this sunny though chilly late February day. The box here had twenty-six levers with two spare; the biggest frame of all the boxes on the line. A level crossing was located just north of the box. J39 No.64816 had the honour of working the final parcels service over the route on the following day; part of its duty was hauling a number of open wagons which were left along the route for collection during March. *J.W.Armstrong (ARPT).*

The grandiose architecture of Wooperton greets us on that February day in 1953. Looking for all intents like a working station, it's difficult to believe that twenty-three years had passed since its closure. This was another station equipped in 1901 with a dwarf signal frame and the same type of timber design employed at Glanton has been used for the building to house the frame; note the name board, and the shunting pole on the erstwhile garden, as for the empty bottle! The overbridge carried the B6346 road. On route to this place we crossed over what was probably the most spectacular man-made structure on the line, the wrought-iron lattice girder bridge spanning the River Breamish on the level stretch of track immediately north of Hedgeley box. *J.W.Armstrong (ARPT)*.

The undulating glacial-carved landscape just south of Ilderton as seen from the footplate of No.62371 on the Ilderton-Alnwick working during the afternoon of 27th February 1953. The A697 road is just beyond the hedges on the right. *J.W.Armstrong (ARPT)*.

Ilderton became the terminus of the southern end of the line in 1949 and No.62371 has already run round the stock and is now awaiting the loading operation of goods and parcels into one of the vans further along the platform. The twenty-two lever signal box has a typical stone base found at other boxes along the line; entrance was via a short stairway off the platform. Of interest are the sleepers on the loop line. They consist mainly of concrete blocks with timber sleepers used intermittently at the rail joints and halfway along the length to maintain gauge. *J.W.Armstrong (ARPT)*.

Here is our D20 on arrival at Ilderton. The 4-4-0 is essentially at the end-of-the-line (note the sleeper placed across the track to prevent further northward progress!) and is about to propel its train into the erstwhile station platform prior to running around. *J.W.Armstrong (ARPT)*.

Bridge No.42 at Ilderton used to carry the railway over Lilburn Burn using a 30ft wrought-iron span between stone abutments, at least it did until the night of 25th-26th October 1949 when a rain storm accompanied by very strong winds swept the nearby hills where the streams which fed Lilburn Burn were inundated so that the burn too was overwhelmed. The resultant stream of water scoured the foundations of Bridge No.42 and the north abutment collapsed into the now raging torrent. Nearly four years after the event, the bridge plate remains in place. Although a couple of bridges on the northern section of the line had been badly damaged during the August 1948 floods, they were in fact repaired whereas their damage should have meant the end for the branch. However, the infant BR decided to get the line up and running again along with the other routes in the area which had been affected. By the autumn of 1949 BR's accountants had managed to look at the traffic figures for the A&C line before a decision was made to either repair Bridge No.42 or not. The latter course was chosen and so the line was then worked as two separate railways with Tweedmouth shed supplying the motive power for the Coldstream-Wooler section and Alnmouth shed doing the same for the section from Ilderton. *J.W.Armstrong (ARPT).*

A last look at our train being loaded at Ilderton; before we leave this section of the branch and bridge that gap to Wooler, I wonder just what was being loaded from that flatbed lorry into the van? *J.W.Armstrong (ARPT)*.

This is Wooler, the largest and busiest of the intermediate stations on the branch which was to be expected as it served the largest community (pop. 1,577 souls in 1937) although it too had closed in September 1930 as the LNER grappled with their finances. This is the Down platform buildings on which nothing had been spared during construction. The cost of the Wooler station including the waiting shed on the Up platform came to £2,856 whereas most of the other station buildings on the line which were standardised, either left or right depending on situation, cost £1,686 each or even cheaper as at Edlingham for instance. *Roy Stevens.*

(*opposite, top*) An undated image of the Up platform at Wooler with its waiting shed. We are looking north on what is again a rather pleasant day. After closure as a passenger station the waiting shed became the male accommodation for a Youth Hostel Association facility from 1932 to 1939. *Roy Stevens.* (*opposite, bottom*) Wooler station in June 1958 with a batch of new 16-ton steel mineral wagons stabled on the Up platform line! *J. Mallon (NERA).*

(*opposite, top*) Wooler was provided with two signal boxes, North and South. This is Wooler North at an unrecorded date but appearing to be still operational. This particular box controlled the gates over the A611 which road linked Wooler with Berwick-on-Tweed. Note the carriage landing, an early form of 'car-carrying' whereby the carriages of the toffs were often carried by the railway companies. *J. Mallon NERA.* (*opposite, bottom*) The large goods warehouse at Wooler in 1958 showing wagons inside the facility; by now it appears very quiet. Note a further batch of new 16-ton mineral wagons beyond. *J. Mallon (NERA).*

Another view of Wooler – albeit undated but it's probably about June 1958 – from the south end of the station showing the water tank, and more of those wagons. *J. Mallon (NERA).*

Two level crossings located either side of Akeld: (*opposite, top*) Looking north at Bendor crossing which was located less than a mile east of Akeld. Although bisecting a minor road, the crossing was gated and had a Keeper's house besides the signal box. During the 1920s many of the Crossing Keepers jobs were abolished and the Platelayers wives were given the duty at much reduced rates of pay! (*opposite, bottom*) Yeavering crossing – located west of Akeld – had no gates; the road, from the B6351, led to Coupland less than a mile away. Note the standardised design of the boxes. *Both J. Mallon (NERA).*

Akeld station viewed from the bridge carrying the A697 road where the latter changed direction northwards whilst the railway continued westward. Here we are looking towards Bendor where we have come from. The dwarf frame signal box sticks out from the main veranda like a sore thumb; the original free standing box was located opposite the platform approximately in line with the newer structure. The monolith-like structure in front of the building contained a weighing machine; the weighbridge itself lay in front. The rail entrance to the coal cells were beyond the points to the goods yard. *J.W.Armstrong (ARPT).*

The only sound is the wind rustling the trees! (*above*) The station from lineside circa 1958; note the running-in board waiting just in case a passenger train might appear from nowhere. Apparently the station houses on this line have all managed to survive and have been taken over as private residencies; probably a record if such a thing existed for closed branch lines. (*below*) It is easy to appreciate the attraction of these premises for dwelling houses. Now, how do you like your finials? *Both J. Mallon (NERA).*

(*above*) The aforementioned bridge with its fair share of smoke-blackened stonework! *J. Mallon NERA*. The coal cells (*below*) still in use at this unknown date. An easy modelling project rarely presented; this set has some interesting extra features. *J. Mallon (NERA)*.

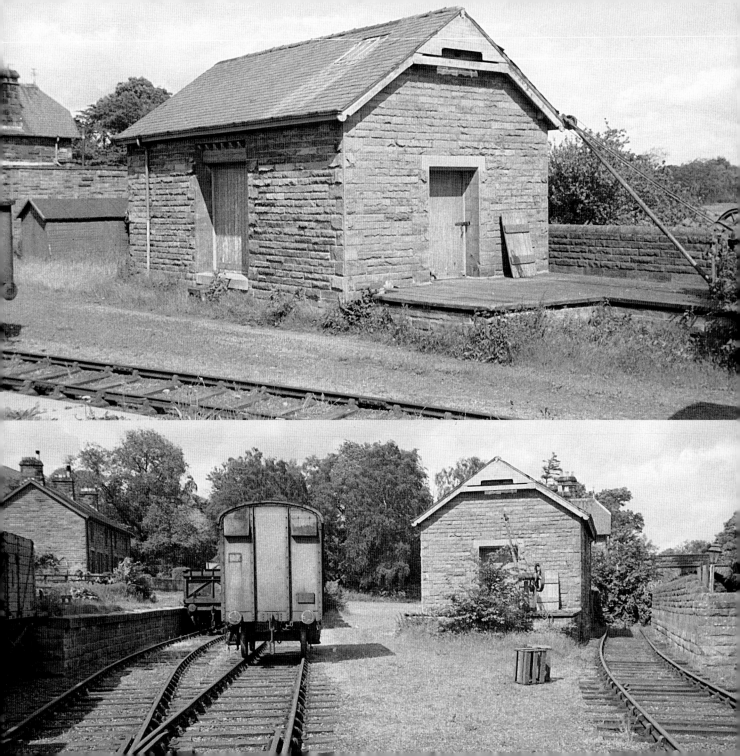

(*opposite*) Two views of the other goods facilities at Akeld with the small warehouse (*top*) and its adjacent dock equipped with a 1-ton hand crane. The general view shows more of the infrastructure and on the left the railway cottages provided for the staff. The coal cells were located to the left of the wooden-bodied open wagon. Closed from 29th March 1965, the place was an idyllic scene and surely ripe for a modelling project. *Both J. Mallon (NERA).*

The erstwhile Kirknewton station on 4th August 1964; we are looking west in our imaginary direction of travel. Although the passenger facilities succumbed to the austerity of 1930, the goods yard remained in operation until the end of March 1953. Some eleven years later the coming and going of the branch trains to Akeld and Wooler have kept the foliage largely away from the track but that was soon to change when in March of 1965 the line was finally closed. It would be interesting to know what BR sold these properties for! *J.W.Armstrong (ARPT).*

(*opposite*) Kirknewton station and signal box from rail side and road side circa 1958. This station building was one of only two single-storey examples on the line – the other being Edlingham – but nevertheless the striking architecture once again lifts this building above the usual. For anyone who has a passion for roofs, this semi-hipped design is superb; topped off with those tall chimney stacks and elaborate finials, it would be a shame to erect a satellite dish! We have travelled just over twenty-seven miles since Alnwick and we are in the ascent once again but only on a reasonable 1 in 110. *J. Mallon (NERA)*.

Looking back at the way we have arrived here at Kilham Sidings (the nameboard is just showing above the wall next to the house). With nearly thirty miles under our belts we are in the valley of the Bowmont Water, a slow flowing stream draining a decent chunk of the Cheviot Hills but with a potential to become a raging torrent causing untold damage as it did in 1948 when it removed a bridge between here and Mindrum. Repairs in 1949 saw the bridge restored and the line re-opened, at least as far as Wooler. Long since demolished, a signal box once graced this location and it stood just to the left of the gates behind the telegraph pole. The sidings to the right had a platform for goods transfer. Right, onward and upward with just one more mile of modest climbing ahead then its downhill all the way to the junction at Coldstream. *J. Mallon (NERA)*.

Mindrum, Tuesday 4th August 1964. Looking overgrown and a tad neglected, the future looked bleak for this former station but with hindsight we know that things turned-out quite differently. Once again a magnificent pile with all the A&C trimmings lavished on the structure. The goods facility here was still active at this date and had a similar layout to that at Akeld with coal cells furthest away from the passenger platform whilst a goods warehouse and sidings lay between. Note the dwarf signal frame building at the front of the veranda; the conventional box it replaced stood just to the right of the photographer. The requirement for trains to pass in the loop here was long gone and its last use passed into history before this image was recorded. This is the final station before Coldstream and we have covered nearly thirty-two miles of the branch thus far; just three more to go. *J.W.Armstrong (ARPT).*

We have reached the end of the line as far as the A&C is concerned: This is Coldstream station which is actually serving Cornhill-on-Tweed (pop. 585 in 1937) in Northumberland, England, rather than Coldstream (pop. 2013 in 1937), Berwickshire, Scotland which is one and a half mile distant north across the River Tweed, not to mention a political border! Opened by the North Eastern Railway in July 1849 as Cornhill, the name was changed in October 1873. Closed to passenger traffic from 15th June 1964, Coldstream closed to goods traffic from 29th March 1965. This undated image was probably recorded in 1964, perhaps even on the final day of working, Saturday 13th June; it was captured in the morning and is looking south from whence we came. This station was typical early NER with low platforms and a bay-windowed station house on the Up platform with adjoining passenger facilities; the footbridge is a standard NE design, as is the tall signal box. After closure this site was cleared and the place is now a housing estate. *J.W.Armstrong (ARPT)*.

NEWCASTLE – BLYTH

We are now about to travel from Manors to Blyth using steam traction for the whole journey. Looking at the blossom on the trees its early morning in spring and the station clock appears to be correct. We are stood on Trafalgar Street, Manors, about to walk over to the station and book our day-return to Blyth. Road traffic is light, very light and it may well be a Sunday; note the parking meters already in situ; its early 1960s but when exactly? *Ken Groundwater (ARPT)*.

Cl.4 No.42085 and G5 No.67347 heading or about to head trains on the Blyth & Tyne platform (4 & 5). The date is 19th April 1952, a Saturday which was ideal for travelling around the system as there were fewer commuters and just as many trains. The Cl.4 was a fairly recent arrival at Heaton but by July it was gone. In the meantime it was employed on passenger services to Blyth amongst others. *J.W.Armstrong (ARPT).*

(*left*) G5 No.67326 runs into Benton with five bogies on 5th July 1952.
J.W.Armstrong (ARPT).

(*bottom*) No.67347 crosses over the ECML at Benton Quarry with an afternoon service for Blyth on 5th July 1952. *J.W.Armstrong (ARPT)*.

An unidentified V3 has just arrived from Manors at the one-platform Seghill station on an unrecorded date. We are in mining country now and the subsidence is readily visible. The station here dates from 1841; it managed to get in its centenary and more with its 2nd November 1964 closure. *J.W.Armstrong (ARPT).*

Busy period at Seghill level crossing with an unidentified J27 approaching with a loaded train whilst two Coal Board 0-6-0 saddle tanks wait their turn to cross the A190 road en route to Backworth. Seghill Colliery with its three winding towers dominates the horizon. The date – 1st June 1966 and just behind is Blyth the sea port with staiths on both sides of the river. Of course Blyth handled coal, lots of coal, and the port opened further staiths in 1928. The early-1960s saw the exports peak at 6.9 million tonnes, making Blyth the leading coal shipping port in Europe at that time (the South Wales bubble had burst long beforehand). Besides the staiths on the north bank of the river, British Coal built and opened a new coal loading terminal at Bates, on the south bank just west of Blyth, on 5th April 1991; even after the disastrous industrial action of the 1980s and the closures which followed, optimism still reined with some people! However, the once very productive Northumberland pits were being worked-out and from the fifty coal mines operating in the B&T area during WWI, the final deep mine, at Ellington was closed in 2005. *L.G.Charlton.*

One of the three winding towers used at Seghill Colliery when it was in full production. The Colliery closed in 1962 but the adjacent washery remained operational until into the 1970s. This June 1966 image shows that the winding ropes – cables – have been removed from this headgear but everything else appears intact albeit suffering from subsidence with cracks affecting most of the structures. Opened in 1826, this pit was one of the earliest in the area and at its most productive period some 1,125 men were employed lifting more than 400,000 tons of saleable coal per annum. *L.G.Charlton collection.*

Mining subsidence was responsible for a lot of damage to surface buildings and BR – being in the thick of it – was as liable as anyone to suffer as here at Seaton Deleval station in 1952 where the road bridge carrying the A192 has been shored-up with some hefty kit. *J.W.Armstrong (ARPT)*.

On a glorious summer evening, G5 No.67339 propels its train onto the Avenue branch at Hartley circa 1956. Running between Blyth and Monkseaton (we covered the branch in Northumberland Branch Line:1) these push-pull trains continued until DMUs took over in 1958. Note the tidy station, track and potential garden displays. *J.W.Armstrong (ARPT)*.

This is a Monkseaton-Blyth working which has just departed from Hartley and the signalman is waiting to receive the staff from No.67323's fireman. The little signal box was replaced at some time in the late 1950s by a box erected on the Avenue branch platform at Hartley. We'll stay with this train to Newsham. *J.W.Armstrong (ARPT).*

(*opposite, top*) An unidentified G5 runs into Newsham with a late evening train from Manors to Blyth circa 1956. This station marks the dividing of the ways for trains to Bedlington and Newbiggin (*see also* NBL: 1) and those to Blyth. (*opposite, bottom*) Working back to town from Blyth, G5 No.67295 calls at Newsham with a Manors train circa 1956. *J.W.Armstrong (ARPT).*

(*above*) We have arrived at our destination – Blyth where we meet the G5 which was different! No.67340 is inspected by its Driver after working a push-pull service into Blyth from Monkseaton in 1954. *P.J. Robinson.* (*left*) This innovative platform seat would probably win design awards nowadays and would cost goodness knows how much to purchase if you were so inclined. When it was made in 1867 it was probably one of many with the size dictated by the length of name board; it may of course be younger than that but a new station was constructed at Blyth during that year replacing an earlier establishment from 1847. Closure took place from 2nd November 1964, long before steam was withdrawn from many of the workings in the area. *Roy Stevens.*

It was a period when rail tours were running seemingly every weekend, some for longer than the usual day-out. This is the joint *RCTS-SLS NORTH EASTERN TOUR* 1963 which ran over a number of days visiting what appeared to be every branch, freight-only line, and secondary line in the NE Region. On Sunday 29th September Blyth was one of the destination branches and Ivatt Cl.4 No.43057 is doing the honours and is seen prior to departure from the station. For those who could afford the expense, and the time, this was the tour to be on. Happy days! *I.S.Carr (ARPT)*.

Two extremes from the transition period of the 1960s: The manual coaling stage at South Blyth MPD on Tuesday 17th September 1963 with J27 No.65838 being serviced. This stage dates from the opening of the shed in 1880 and had undergone a number of attempts to clad the structure to make it more comfortable for the coalmen facing those biting easterly winds straight off the North Sea; the corrugated iron cladding was the last material used and was still employed in 1967 when the depot closed. *George Ives.* In total contrast, a Diesel Multiple Unit consisting a 4-car Derby Lightweight set departs from Blyth terminus on 8th August 1963 destination Newcastle. *C.J.B.Sanderson (ARPT).*

(*top, bottom left and bottom right*) Keeping up with our trait of featuring rolling stock for those with an interest, we present three BR Instruction Coaches temporarily residing at South Blyth MPD on 17th September 1963 – DE320043, DE951650, DE961800. Their origins were ex-NER; unknown; ex-NBR, respectively. *All George Ives.*

THE MORPETH – REEDSMOUTH – ROTHBURY LINE (The Wannie!)

Starting this section on a melancholy note, we present G5 No.67341 at Morpeth station on Saturday 13th September 1952 in charge of the last train to Rothbury – the 5-50 p.m. arriving Rothbury 6-58 p.m. The gentleman from whose collection this image has materialised is pictured here as a very young budding enthusiast: Michael Halbert, front far right. Suitably decorated, the 0-4-4T was one of South Blyth's stud and although the 52F shedplate denoted North Blyth, BR did not differentiate between the two depots by giving them separate shed codes and therefore both fell under one! *M.Halbert collection.*

Morpeth running-in board 1939; change for all those places and more. The junction at Morpeth was built up slowly during the nineteenth century from the station being opened in March 1847, along with its section of what became the ECML, to the opening of the Blyth & Tyne connection from Hepscott exactly ten years later. Next was the line to Scotsgap (note the 1939 rendering of that name; it seems that BR finally got rid of the gap which had been redundant since October 1903; perhaps the board pre-dated 1903?) in July 1862 which joined up with Reedsmouth in May 1865. Finally, the line to Rothbury which when proposed was to go on to Coldstream or rather Cornhill to keep the route in England, but didn't make it and had to make do with Rothbury as its terminus. That branch was realised on 1st November 1870 but was never going to be what the promoters had initially wished. Rothbury had an engine shed from opening and during its eighty-odd colourful years of existence it housed two locomotives for working the branch. Of course we haven't mentioned who initially owned what once the dust had settled so please allow us to indulge you. The B&T became part of the NER in 1874 and that marriage upset the North British who had ideas of their own to cosy-up to the B&T as a means of getting into Newcastle the back-way not to mention access to the very productive coalfield north of the Tyne. The North British had indeed invested in Northumberland during the 1860s with the branch from Riccarton to Hexham via Reedsmouth; then the somewhat covert change of direction from Reedsmouth towards Morpeth and the hoped-for B&T. So, leaving the ECML behind let us strike out and get on our way towards Rothbury. *M.Halbert collection.*

Our first station is Meldon some five miles or so from Morpeth. The platform is on the north side of the line with goods facilities east of the station. Evidence of platform lengthening by the North British can be seen with the timber extensions. What the NBR did do at the planning stage was include provision for doubling the single line with all the bridges and embankments suitably ready. This image was recorded in August 1954 when the passenger services had been stopped for almost two years; signage was still evident on the station building although it is informing of a public telephone which was possibly the only one in the immediate community then. *C.J.B.Sanderson (ARPT)*.

What a difference eight years can make! (*opposite, top*) Meldon station looking west on 5th June 1955 with everything looking fairly reasonable less than three years after passenger services were withdrawn. *L.G.Charlton collection.* (*opposite*) From virtually the same vantage point on 27th September 1963, the run down was nearly complete but goods trains still ran over these metals as did excursions. No fancy gardens at this end of the line note. In July 1962 a test was carried out with a Sulzer Type 2 diesel-electric Bo-Bo over the ex-NBR branches from Morpeth to Rothbury and Bellingham resulting in permission being granted by the Civil Engineer for their use over the routes subject to a speed of 35 m.p.h. *John Boyes (ARPT)*.

(*opposite, top*) Angerton station from the south-east on 8th August 1954. For literally miles around there was nothing but isolated farms and the homes of the gentry yet this place along with other stations on the line managed to exist until after WWII. In 1951 this station issued 291 tickets which is less than one a day even allowing for Sunday closures! Something of a garden has been created here near the waiting room; I suppose the staff needed something to do between intending passengers. *C.J.B.Sanderson (ARPT)*. (*opposite, bottom*) Angerton from its eastern end with the level crossing prominent; taken from a passing train at an unknown date, the Gateman can be seen making his way to open them once again for the public road users. *M.Halbert collection.*

(*above*) The erstwhile Middleton North station looking east 8th August 1954. The suffix was added by the LNER immediately after Grouping to avoid confusion with their other Middleton's in Yorkshire and Norfolk (not to mention a couple of LMS examples too). This is not the original station in that its location east of the road bridge prevented lengthening of its meagre 40 yards long platform so this 90 yards example was built west of the bridge. Note the small wooden platform building. The loop which was latterly made into a siding, served the goods platform. *C.J.B.Sanderson (ARPT).*

(*right*) This is the NBR enamel Trespass Notice located at Meldon station but similar to any found at the stations along the Wansbeck Valley line. This particular example was photographed on 27th September 1963 and considering its age is in remarkable condition. *John Boyes (ARPT).*

J27 No.65819 works a livestock special at Scotsgap circa 1960 with a very young 'Fireman' looking out of the cab. This particular 0-6-0 had been resident at North Blyth since March 1943 but ended its days working from South Blyth after September 1963 to withdrawal in October 1966. Remaining local to the very end, it was cut-up at Hughes, Bolckow, in North Blyth. Now the circular building in the right background with that wonderful roof is not the fabled long-lost Scotsgap locomotive roundhouse pre-dating the Rothbury shed; at least I hope not! It was the livestock auction mart. *S.C.Crook (ARPT)*.

A general view of Scotsgap station and goods yard on 8th August 1958; as with all the stations on this line – Morpeth–Reedsmouth and Scotsgap–Rothbury – passenger services were withdrawn from Monday 15th September 1952. However, the cessation of goods facilities occurred in two stages with the majority succumbing from 11th November 1963 but Knowesgate, Scotsgap, and Woodburn hanging on until 3rd October 1966. This image captured from the bridge carrying the B6343 over the railway is looking south-east with J25 No.65727 ready for some shunting whilst on the platform a Border Collie ignores proceedings as something else requires its attention. Immediately south-west of the station along the aforementioned B-road is Cambo (pop. 89 in 1937), the nearest, and largest, settlement it seems for some distance around. The signal box nameplate displays Scotsgap Junction! *I.S.Carr (ARPT)*.

J21 No.65119 approaches Scotsgap station with a passenger train from the Reedsmouth direction on an unrecorded date in the 1950s. From 23rd December 1951 to 14th September 1952 this 0-6-0 was allocated to Reedsmouth shed so the chances are this image dates from the summer 1952. We are looking north-west from beneath the B6343 overbridge towards the junction with the line to Rothbury which leaves this formation immediately after that footbridge in the distance. On the right, much nearer the camera is the locomotive refuge siding complete with 18ft. engine pit and 45ft. turntable for the use of the branch engine which in this case was the motive power from Reedsmouth not Rothbury. This view also affords us a look into a future which didn't happen but if it had this is what the 'Wannie' would have looked like throughout had those NBR plans been totally realised. However, even though the NBR had something of a parsimonious reputation regarding station accommodation, they certainly invested in facilities for the motive power on this line with two engine sheds and three turntables. Of course, it was the former North Eastern Area of the LNER which inherited all of these assets but never did anything to improve them. *K.H.Cockerill (ARPT)*.

This is Woodburn the last proper station before Reedsmouth; to get here from Scotsgap we have passed through Knowesgate which served the village of Kirkwhelpington over a mile to the south of the station, Parsons Platform, a private platform used by the Parson's family, and Summit Cottages where no platform existed but stops were made to pick up the wives of railway personnel who had homes in the area. The opening of the line to Rothbury and the introduction of direct services from Morpeth to that place put the Reedsmouth-Scotsgap line into a branch status as far as passenger traffic was concerned. This undated image was obviously recorded during a summer and perusal of the station platform leads us to the fact that the station was still operational, the goods yard certainly so with a new steel-bodied 16-ton mineral wagon present; perhaps 1950 would be a reasonable date? The main road is the A68, built here over a Roman road which explains the straight sections. We are looking northwards and over the hill where the A68 disappears is the Otterburn military training area. That particular establishment brought lots of special workings to this branch both before and after it was closed to passenger traffic. The line from Morpeth to Woodburn continued in use for military trains until 1966 with some carrying equipment and others personnel. Type 2 diesel locomotives were by then hauling much of the military traffic alongside J27s. Today the station buildings have been incorporated into a dwelling house, complete with platform. *M.Halbert collection.*

J27 No.65842 heads the last Morpeth–West Woodburn pick-up freight in September 1966. *P.J. Robinson.*

58 Close-up of Woodburn station from beneath the road bridge, 15th July 1952. *C.J.B.Sanderson (ARPT).*

If we were on an imaginary train from Woodburn to Reedsmouth, we would have been enjoying a descent which started at Summit Cottages and which in places became a hairy 1 in 62. We have been following the contours shaped through the hills by the River Rede and about a mile or so from Reedsmouth a siding appears on our left. The siding is in fact a bit more than that and is the remnant of another branch line which initially served a couple of quarries at Broomhope (Craig and Hindhaugh) but has latterly been a means of getting equipment and supplies to a weapons testing area owned by industrialist W.G.Armstrong. The last minerals were taken from the quarries to Armstrong's Elswick works in 1879 and the landscape features which were left behind made a superb range for testing large calibre gun barrels to be fitted on ships of the Royal Navy – and probably others too. This undated image shows J25 No.65727 (allocated to South Blyth from March 1955 to withdrawal in January 1961; oh yes, it was one of those which worked on the GWR for six years during WW2) shunting the branch having left the rest of its train on the main line and securely pinned down looking at that gradient; the branch extended about a mile south-eastwards following the course of Broomhope Burn. We are looking north-easterly in the direction of Woodburn but the high ground of Chesterhope Common dominates the background. This whole area has military connections going back almost two–thousand years; the Romans had a fort – called Habitancvm – beside the Rede near Woodburn whilst another was located near Steel just west of the A68, another Roman road called Dere Street. *John. Spencer.Gilks,*

This is what was at the end of the aforementioned branch – The Steel. Fashioned from a quarry, this industrial site was created to test gun barrels before they were installed into warship turrets. Nearest the camera we can see the gantry used to set-up the barrels for firing and beneath are two what look like 14-inch barrels, a popular calibre in British battleships during the First World War and into WW2. These precision made yet robust pieces of metal usually weighed in excess of 100-tons not including the breech mechanism. Every barrel manufactured at the Elswick works was brought by rail to this place for testing prior to fitting into the turrets of the warship being fitted-out in the shipyard. Besides those battleships built on Tyneside, many of those built at Barrow-in-Furness also had their gun barrels made at Elswick works and later tested here. It would be interesting to know just how big the butts were into which the inert shells were fired. Obviously annoying the neighbours with excessive noise was not something to worry about as those nearest to this installation, about a mile away, probably worked here anyway. However, next time you go for a walk in the country don't think it's all bogs, rocky outcrops and serene valleys. Take a good look for any industrial archaeology which may or may not be obvious. This particular set-up was run-down shortly after battleships became unpopular and by 1960 the place was closed but I should imagine something survives? *M.Halbert collection.*

(*top*) Military special or a garden excursion? Two J21s and eight bogies near Reedsmouth, date unknown. *K.H.Cockerill (ARPT)*. (*above*) Alongside the Reedsmouth water tower, J21 No.65042 stands waiting for the 7-44 a.m. departure time with the Scotsgap train on Saturday 13th September 1952. Arrival at Scotsgap would be 8-18 a.m. some four minutes ahead of the arrival of the Rothbury to Morpeth train which departed Scotsgap at 8-25 a.m. for a 8-51 a.m. arrival in Morpeth in time to catch an Up express which arrived Newcastle 9-29 a.m. All rather civilised, assuming good time-keeping. On the Hexham-bound platform, the 7-48 a.m. departure from Reedsmouth to Hexham, 6-47 a.m. ex-Riccarton Junction, would arrive Hexham at 8-27 a.m. in time to catch a connection to Newcastle for a 9-7 a.m. arrival. Twenty-two minutes difference, one change or two? Decisions! I think it was Tommy Trinder who coined the phrase 'You Lucky People!' *J.W.Armstrong (ARPT)*.

We have doubled-back to Scotsgap, or at least the junction for the Rothbury branch and have now proceeded north along the branch and climb steadily at 1 in 75 towards Longwitton, our first station and the summit of the route at just below 700ft. Looking over the parapet of the B6342 road bridge we get a better view of the station from this elevation. Originally called Rothley, the station was private for the use of the local gentry when opened in November 1870 but by 1873 it was brought into public use and then two years later had a name change to Longwitton in April 1875. The original platform layout did not include the coach body which was a later addition becoming a useful store. This 15th July 1952 image of the station is looking due east over empty Northumbrian landscape. Various minerals have been quarried or mined in this area over the decades and Longwitton was located near a drift mine which produced saleable coal for a number of years and which was hauled away by rail via the small goods yard behind the main station building but those fleeting glory days are long gone. Of interest here are the concrete sleepers laid down from this end of the platform in the Rothbury direction. Just how far they were laid is unknown but more to the point, why were they laid there at all with one goods train a day and the occasion excursion? Or was it the weather test which up here is a reasonable test area with some vicious winters. If you know anything about these sleepers then please tell us as we too would like to know. Right, with some three miles under our belts it is onward to Ewesley about two miles away. *C.J.B.Sanderson (ARPT)*

(top) The Driver of G5 No.67341 is on the phone to the signalman at Ewesley on 13th September 1952. Note more concrete sleepers! *J.W.Armstrong (ARPT)*. *(above)* Ewesley station on 15th July 1952 looking tired, and ready for retirement, another timber building with austerity in mind for everything else too. The NBR did not lavish too much on these intermediate stations but they were allowed to build where they wanted it seems because this station was located right in the middle of an ancient hill fort; imagine that happening today!!!!. Once again, concrete sleepers everywhere. *C.J.B.Sanderson (ARPT)*.

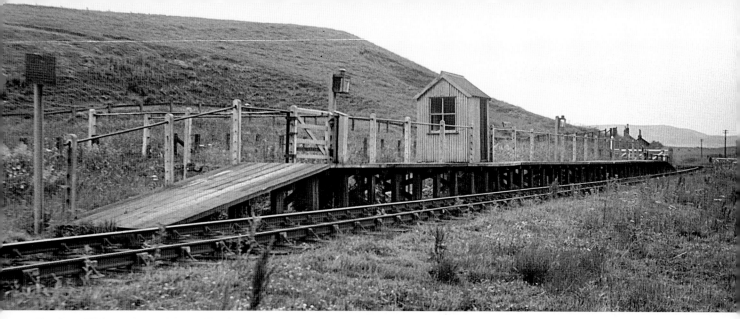

Fontburn Halt was located immediately north-east of Font Reservoir, the latter being responsible for the existence of the former which was constructed for the convenience of construction workers who lived in a temporary 'town' or 'shanty' from 1901 to 1909 whilst the damming of the river Font and construction of a reservoir took place. Apparently some 450 people lived in the 'shanty-town' but nearby was a lime works served by a quarry – White House quarry – whose workers also enjoyed the use of the halt which came into operation in January 1903 and besides the 80-yard long timber platform, it had a waiting shed along with a booking office – who said the NBR Directors were 'tight?' The quarry and lime works had been established about 1896 and trains were calling there unofficially to pick-up and set down workers. The Halt which was originally called 'Temporary Platform at Whitehouse Siding' for Workmen' was renamed Fontburn in May 1904 to avoid confusion with Whitehouse in Aberdeenshire. During the seventeen months from coming into operation to being renamed, the platform had been inspected by the B-o-T and duly given its station status to serve passengers. Just before Grouping the NBR closed the station (the construction people had gone by 1910) but a petition was presented to the Board who lamented and within a month of closure the place was reopened but as an unstaffed Halt – everyone was happy. This was the halt on 15th July 1952 viewed from the south-east; today nothing remains of the structure but the reservoir is still in operation. *C.J.B.Sanderson (ARPT)*.

This tiny Hunslet 0-4-0ST, named TYNEMOUTH, was used during the construction of the Font project. *J.W.Armstrong Miscellany (ARPT)*.

Having been unstaffed since September 1948, Brinkburn lost its station status for its final four years and became a Halt. This is the place on 15th July 1952 looking very tidy but the doorway in the gable end has been bricked-up; the running-in board is still in situ. A small goods yard was located behind the buildings but even in 1952 it didn't look as though it had seen any traffic for a while. Notices advised intending passengers to purchase tickets from the guard on the train and those with parcels to forward should go to Rothbury. The erstwhile station was just over two miles short of Rothbury clinging to a position on a hill overlooking Coquet Dale. Once again there was no sign of any communities within walking distance other than Rothbury. The river which gave the dale its name lies in the wooded valley below the hill. We are looking north at the remnants of what was Rothbury Forest which once covered all of these hills. Note the curvature of the railway which has followed the contours of the high ground since Scotsgap; it was these curves which were partly responsible for an accident in the winter of 1897 when a train with 250 people on board exceeded the 30 m.p.h limit and at 47 m.p.h. the leading coach left the rails at points near Rothbury and then fell on its side. The accident left three people dead and twenty-one injured. The train was returning from Newcastle after the passengers had attended a Pantomime but had been delayed en route. By the time it got to Scotsgap it was already some 95 minutes late. The other vehicles in the train were all derailed but luckily there were no casualties therein. *C.J.B.Sanderson (ARPT).*

J21 No.65110 runs onto the 42ft. turntable at Rothbury on Saturday 13th April 1957. This was a Heaton based engine and had worked in on an excursion from Newcastle for Rothbury Races; it's a bit early in the season for the gardening fraternity but those Townies out for a breath of fresh air and a brisk walk would have found the trip to Rothbury worthwhile. The gable of the by now disused engine shed can be seen behind the blowing-off steam. The original shed opened with the line in 1870 but two years later a fire destroyed it and a new shed was required; fire struck again in 1915 but damage was minimal this time. At closure, which was on the same day as the passenger workings ceased, the allocation consisted of two locomotives, G5 No.67341 (a stand-in for No.67296) and J21 No.65035, much the same as it had in NBR days. At Grouping D51 NB1401 was allocated and had been for many years until it was condemned in October 1924; it was never replaced by another 4-4-0T but Reedsmouth shed housed sister NB1402 until it too was condemned in September 1925. J36 No.9791 was another long-time resident at Rothbury and it transferred to Reedsmouth on 7th October 1933 to be replaced by former North Eastern motive power in the shape of J21 No.877 which lasted until condemned in May 1944 but was replaced by sister J21 No.1557 from Blaydon; it moved on to West Auckland on 6th February 1949. Another J21, No.5035, arrived 18th July 1948 and was there to the end when it transferred to Heaton. G5 No.1918 (67296) came on 23rd November 1940 and stayed to the end whereas No.2086 (67315) arrived from Heaton on 13th May 1936 but transferred to Alston on 29th May 1940. Whenever a gap occurred in the supply of motive power, South or North Blyth would lend either four-coupled tanks or six-coupled tender engines. *D.Fairley (ARPT)*.

Rothbury terminus 15th July 1952; the last summer for passenger trains and two months from cessation! Before Grouping the branch had four return passenger trains a day with five on a Saturday but the LNER and later BR dropped the number to just two workings a day with three on Saturdays but latterly the extra Saturday train was dropped too. Freight remained steady at one train a day and that managed to keep the branches open into the 1960s at least. Sheep sales at Rothbury during market days could bring as many as a hundred wagons into the terminus for loading; although the livestock market was near the station, I should imagine organised chaos reigned with Border Collies everywhere! The passenger platform was 200 yards long and all the station facilities were at the western – terminal – end where a turntable served the engine shed and a small shed for a ganger's vehicle. A signal box stood at the east end of the platform just behind the photographer. Goods facilities spread out to the north of the platform. Except for the enlarged engine shed, this whole terminus was little changed from its 1st November 1870 opening but note the seemingly compulsory coach body which was retro-installed at an unknown date. Most stations on the line from Morpeth have one of these grounded vehicles which found a myriad of uses over the years. *C.J.B.Sanderson (ARPT)*.

As we saw on page 48, the last passenger train to Rothbury on that fateful Saturday 13th September 1952 was hauled by G5 No.67341 which was sub-shedded at Rothbury. That same locomotive had hauled the final passenger train – the 4-30 p.m. – from the town and is seen at the head of the two-coach load. To help 'celebrate' the event the Stationmaster and his family along with the engine crew posed for photographers prior to departure. The chalked legend on the message board reads 'Cheerio Rothbury 1872-1952 Good Luck.' Of course that last figure of the first date was wrong and should read 1870 but in the circumstances we can easily forgive the writer. The G5 worked through to Morpeth to then perform that last working at depicted on page 48. The Reedsmouth to Scotsgap last train – 4-15 p.m. ex-Reedsmouth, arrive Scotsgap 4-48 p.m. in time to connect with the working from Rothbury which arrived 5-01 p.m. – and return working was hauled by J21 No.65042, the 0-6-0 returning to shed overnight at Reedsmouth. both images *J.W.Armstrong (ARPT)*.

TRAFALGAR YARD – QUAYSIDE BRANCH

Hauling a train of timber, ES1 No.26501 emerges into the daylight at Trafalgar yard after traversing the short tunnel linking the yard to another tunnel connecting to the quay on the north bank of the River Tyne known as the Quayside branch; J77 No.68440 runs into the picture from the east. The yard here was just to the east of Manors station and adjacent to the ECML where the latter was crossed by one of Newcastle's main thoroughfares – New Bridge Street – which in this view from 1954 was still carrying trolleybuses along with the associated catenary. The Heaton based Bo-Bo, along with sister No.26500 were the only two members of the class introduced in 1905 by the North Eastern specifically to work this branch with its difficult curvature and steep incline all set in a half-mile long tunnel. Inside the tunnel section the electric locomotives collected power from a third-rail but in the open air at both ends, overhead lines provided power through a pantograph on the cab roof. No.26501 has just extended its pantograph and the end of the third-rail can be seen by the first set of wheels of the leading wagon. Note the signals located to the right of that first wagon. The cabin at the tunnel mouth, with shunting poles in abundance, was used to control the coming and going of the trains through the tunnel. *J.W.Armstrong (ARPT)*.

No.26501 again but now sporting the apple-green lined livery bestowed by BR; the date is 3rd August 1963, a Saturday, and 0-6-0DM D2334 along with others of her type have taken over from the J77 steam locomotives on the shunting duties at both Trafalgar yard and on the Quayside. This point seems to be a good place to plot a potted history and description of the branch: A short – 1,306 yards – freight only branch line was opened by the NER in 1873 to connect Trafalgar South goods yard with the Newcastle Corporation quays on the north bank of the River Tyne. Most of the branch was contained in three tunnels which traversed through 180 degrees so that trains entered from the west and then exited to the west at the other end. Not only was the branch severely curved, it was also steeply inclined at 1 in 25 whereby during its passage it descended some 130 feet from the ECML to the Quayside yard on the river. In 1905 the NER decided to electrify the branch and two dedicated locomotives were built to work the trains. Steam was still required on the Quayside for shunting and also in Trafalgar yard but the motive power in the tunnels was exclusively electric. Special brake vans were provided and one of them ran away circa 1963 and crashed in Quayside yard! Of the three tunnels required, the first two from Trafalgar yard were short, the second tunnel beginning at Ingham Place bridge and this then ran into a cutting – surrounded by terraced housing in a district named Battle Field, a childhood haunt of both my parents – which was also on a curve prior to burrowing into the third and longest tunnel beneath St Ann's Yard. *A.Ives (ARPT)*.

Another Saturday afternoon at 'close-of-play' and this time No.26500 is waiting to run back to Heaton. Although at the tunnel entrance, the pantograph of the ES1 has not been raised as a yet-to-arrive diesel shunter would be providing the motive power for the trip so no need for overhead current collection which outside the yard did not exist anyway. Note that the signals have changed from those illustrated on page 69; also the deserted cabin; the date – 27th April 1963. *Brain Ives (ARPT)*.

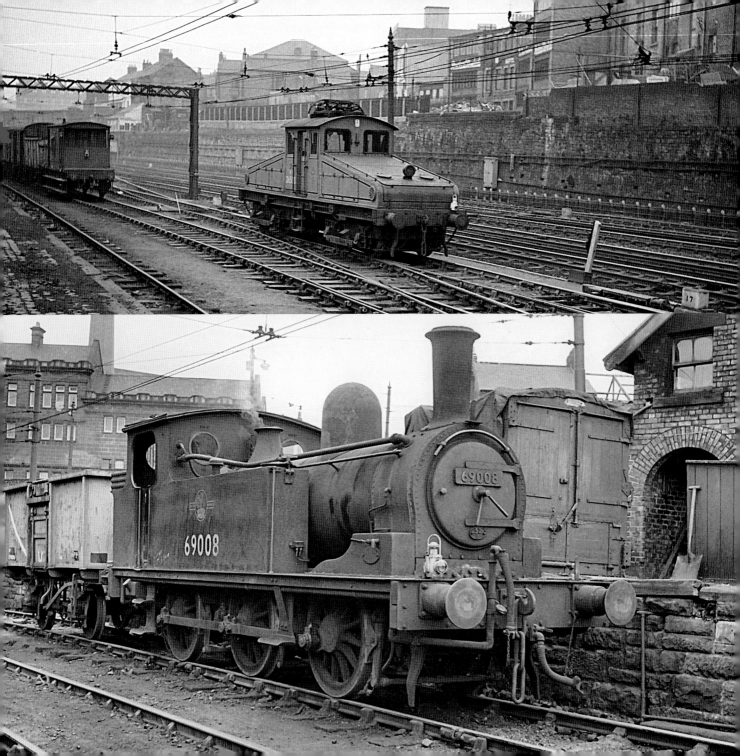

(opposite, top) A week earlier on 20th April, No.26500 was again awaiting a tow to Heaton but is this time is a little further west up the yard. Everything is ready for the trip with pantograph stowed-away, tail-lamp positioned. With the ECML appearing rather quiet. *(opposite, bottom)* The diesel-mechanical diesels might have muscled-in at Trafalgar yard but in this Saturday 25th May 1963 image J72 No.69008 is doing the shunting it seems. Equipped with vacuum ejector and steam heating (from January 1957) the now Heaton based 0-6-0T has been relegated from carriage stock movements and was working its final days with the Goods Department. Not yet fourteen-years old, No.69008 was transferred to Gateshead just three weeks after this image was recorded but with no prospect of any meaningful and long lasting employment it was condemned on 9th December 1963. *Both A.Ives (ARPT)*.

It's the last day of February 1964; once again a Saturday. There is not a soul around Trafalgar yard as No.26500 stands with its pantograph extended but the adjacent unidentified diesel shunter appears to be 'not-too-well' with one of its engine compartment doors ajar. Trolley wires are still spanning New Bridge Street. *I.S.Carr (ARPT)*.

Further detail of the Quayside branch tunnel-end at Trafalgar yard with No.26500 nearing the end of the third-rail but yet to extend the pantograph; it was a two-man job with one to extend the pantograph via a handle in the roof whilst the other picked-up the shoes from the third-rail. The signals are similar to those used at marshalling yards and each show two aspects in this case although their actual working is beyond this compiler. Note the 350 h.p. 0-6-0 DE shunter on the right. This bore took the branch beneath the main road; the tunnel proper was beyond after another short tunnel and a cutting. The date is 29th February 1964 and by now the electric locomotives go off to South Gosforth depot because Heaton had closed during June of the previous year. However, time was running out for the electric traction and both of the Bo-Bo's were condemned on 13th September 1964. *I.S.Carr (ARPT)*.

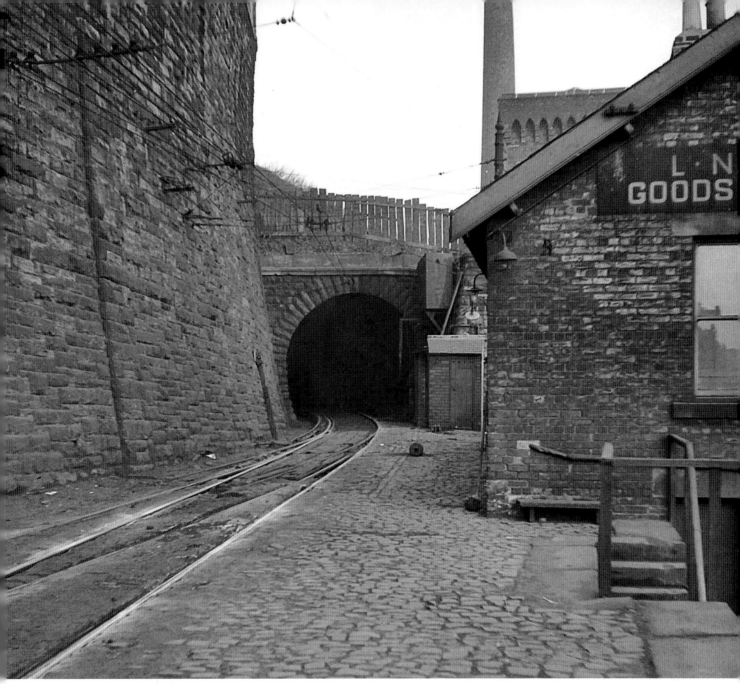

The bottom end of the tunnel; the curvature and indeed the inclination of the line can be clearly seen in this post-war view. Just like the upper (high level) end of the tunnel, the third-rail ends beyond the portal whilst the overhead catenary is waiting. A catch point was located at this end of the branch. Note the LNER's simple, sans serif, signage. *J.W.Armstrong (ARPT)*.

No.26501 under the wires at Quayside yard 25th May 1963, with the compulsory brake van coupled-up, and an unidentified 0-6-0T hiding behind; originally numbered 2 by the North Eastern, that number stuck through LNER days to June 1946 when the Thompson renumbering of LNER locomotives gave this Bo-Bo No.6481 (sister No.1 became 6480). BR changed both in April 1948 so that they became part of the electric locomotive number group which started at 20000; our subject became 26501 and its sister 26500. For the record, the ten former NER Shildon–Newport electric locomotives became 26502 to 26511. Anyway, 26501, just like its sister was always overhauled at Gosforth where the electrical expertise of those running and maintaining the north and south Tyneside suburban electric trains was called upon. High mileage was never a problem with the two ES1s, and so major overhauls were infrequent compared with other types. This locomotive had its final General overhaul from 27th June 1961 to 1st March 1962 where it also acquired this NER green lined livery. Its previous major overhaul was in June/July 1954. After withdrawal, both of the ES1s were stored at Hellifield engine shed for some unfathomable reason, with a view to preservation but the luxury of both Bo-Bo's being saved was not to be and only sister 26500 was kept for the National Collection. No.26501 was sold for scrap and was hauled to Choppington in July 1966 to be broken up in August! *A.Ives (ARPT).*

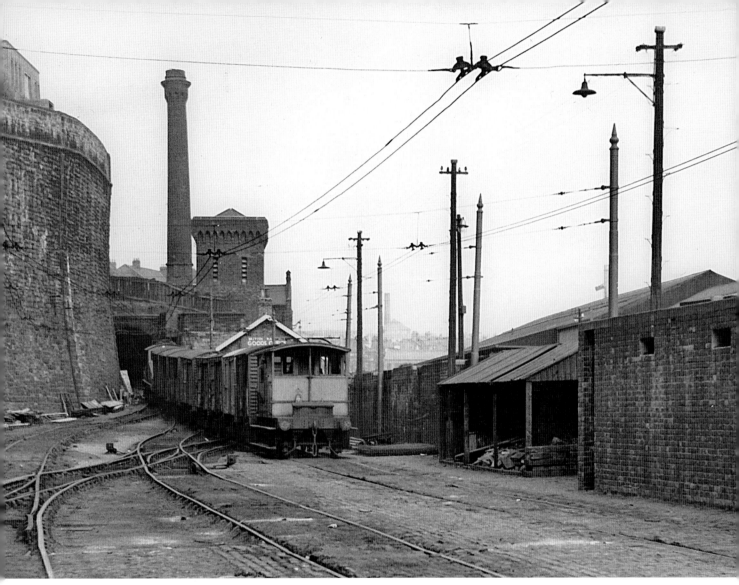

Before the electrics were delivered, steam locomotives worked the branch, L class tanks (LNER J73) were the only engines authorised for use in the tunnel but not beyond. Weighing nearly ten tons more than J71, the J73 was introduced in 1891 specifically for working the inclines on either side of the Tyne and had larger cylinders, coal capacity. The limiting factor on the Quayside (Corporation) lines was the axle weight so only certain classes were allowed there until strengthening work was carried out by 1938. Prior to that date only Y7 and J79 classes were permitted; afterwards J71, J72 and J77 were introduced for the shunting and trip working; J73 had by then left the area for Hull and West Hartlepool. This 7th May 1962 image shows a train about to ascend the branch with the ES1 lowering its pantograph and ready to engage the pick-up shoe to the third rail. The brake van has the large specially fitted sandbox on its platform and two distinctive pipes can be seen leading the sand to the wheels; this equipment was engaged at the start of each descent and the brake van was always leading at the Quayside end of every train. This yard was BR's own property but beyond the walls Newcastle Corporation looked after the railway tracks. *D.R.Dunn collection.*

J72 No.68702 propels a short train into BR's Quayside yard via the eastern gateway circa 1955. The 0-6-0T had joined Heaton's stud in May 1951 and became a regular on these workings. When the electrics were introduced for tasks through the tunnel, the steam shunting engines were brought down from Trafalgar yard each morning to shunt the Quayside and at the end of work each day they were hauled back to Trafalgar yard by one of the electric locomotives. It would be interesting to know what 'strengthening work' was carried out by the Corporation on the Quayside lines in 1938 to enable this class, J71 and J77 to work here. *R.F.Payne (ARPT)*.

The branch emerged at a yard alongside warehouses on Antwerp, Hamburg & Rotterdam Wharf, one of many such wharves situated along the Tyne and which opened in 1870. Newcastle Corporation was responsible for the Quayside and its railway tracks not to mention the roadways which allowed public access in all shapes and forms. This view shows one of the two connections between the BR yard and the Corporation tracks on 5th March 1968 when dilapidation was setting in and the gates were closed for much of the time with little traffic using the branch. The tunnel mouth can be seen in the distance with the BR goods offices guarding the entrance. The Quayside branch closed from 16th June 1969 and another of BR's unusual, if not unique sections of railway passed into history. From this perspective it is easy to appreciate the geography of the branch with its severe difference in elevation between this point alongside the river and Trafalgar yard which was located just to the left (north) of the building on top of the bank. *L.G.Charlton collection.*

And finally: Down on the quay BR also used a road vehicle for shunting and here it is: Registered number HDN 485, BR fleet number ORW 9106 (perhaps), this appears to be a Muir-Hill road tractor (it was probably a Fordson Major converted by Muir-Hill) which was one of the BR motive power items not listed in the Ian Allan ABC although there might have been such a volume for tractors? (If anyone can shed some light on this vehicle please send any information to the publisher via the usual channels – in anticipation, thanks and apologies if any of the numbers are wrong!). Anyway, back to the image which was captured on Saturday morning 25th May 1963 in Quayside yard with three BR personnel stood alongside the trusty steed; two old hands wearing the usual attire afforded long-serving staff in such establishments, although those caps don't appear to be uniform. The other, younger, member of the trio has the BR jacket but has yet to receive the uniform trousers and so wears the more stylish blue jeans with turn-ups. The hands-in-pocket pose reflects the changing attitudes of the period. Now, back to that tractor which has certainly put some hours in pushing wagons about the wharves; the cab is certainly a one-off BR Road Motor Department design with front opening window (modellers note the single screen wiper), sliding side windows and an unusual rear extension in canvas beneath a fixed metal roof which has the BR totem nicely positioned on its front panel. A couple of things worth pondering about this vehicle: where was the exhaust pipe, and obviously that front tyre was beyond its best so how did they get away with it? *A.Ives (ARPT)*.